Measure

Alabama Poetry Series

General Editors: Dara Wier and Thomas Rabbitt

THOMAS SWISS

Measure

The University of Alabama Press

Copyright © 1986 by
The University of Alabama Press
University, Alabama 35486-2877
All rights reserved
Manufactured in the United States of America

Library of Congress Cataloging-in-Publication Data
Swiss, Thomas, 1952-
  Measure.

  (Alabama poetry series)
  I. Title. II. Series.
PS3569.W575M4   1986   811'.54   85-24507
ISBN 0-8173-0292-1 (alk. paper)
ISBN 0-8173-0293-X (pbk. : alk. paper)

for Cynthia

ACKNOWLEDGMENTS

I am grateful to the National Endowment for the Arts for a fellowship that aided me in the completion of this book.

Thanks to Robert Pack and Laurence Lieberman for their thoughtful criticism. Special thanks to Steven Cramer for his advice and encouragement.

Grateful acknowledgment is made to the editors of the following magazines in which these poems appeared:

The Agni Review: "A Virtue of Shape," "Festival Profile," "West Pond Road"
The American Scholar: "The Music Box"
Ascent: "Sunbathers," "Marble," "Then"
Black Warrior Review: "August Outing"
Chelsea: "Waking at Night"
Cimarron Review: "The Wake in the Mansion"
Crazyhorse: "Measure," "In the Late Spring, Cutting Tulips," "Fragments from a Childhood"
The Greensboro Review: "Rilke at Worpswede," "Resting"
The Iowa Review: "Autumnal," "Rounds"
The Literary Review: "Letter from Des Moines," "The Young Couple," "The Drowning"
New England Review/Bread Loaf Quarterly: "Prologue"
Ploughshares: "Journal"
Quarterly West: "Man Waxing Car, 1954"
The Seattle Review: "City Pool"

Some of these poems were reprinted in the *Anthology of Magazine Verse and Yearbook of American Poetry* (Monitor Book Co., Inc., 1980, 1981, 1984) and *Rounds* (Blue Buildings Press, 1982), a limited edition volume.

"Fragments from a Childhood" is for my mother and father.

Contents

III

Prologue

Because I have seen it
  In early Spring,
In Illinois crossing

  The green length
Of lawn, I believe that anything
  I can say about

The wind has already been said.

The ferns know this,
  But I am moved
By their persistence.

  They crowd in close
Rows and, reaching, extend—
  Their swaying

A pledge, a statement of faith.

Now the long view deepens:
  Even God's angels
Admire the wind, especially

  The Fallen, who were
Also His, but who lost their elegant,
  Intricate balance . . .

Night is falling; the light

Closes in. A few colors
  Hang in the mute sky.
And I must walk the ground

With grace, in order
To be recognized as I wish:
Not for my words

But, rather, by my bearing.

I

Letter from Des Moines

And I had forgotten about the stars—
I had been so busy moving again.
From eastern Iowa to central Iowa,
No relief in sight. But stars!
Hundreds—no—thousands of them
On a smoky August night.
And just over the blond chimneys
Of the high-rise housing project—
A constellation. Or I thought so:
Not having a mind for science,
I'm not sure of the proper shapes,
Their illustrative man-made names.
So far away like that,
They often seem unimportant.

At 12, I loved photography
And had a favorite book: an oversized paperback
Called *Trick Shots.* At a gathering of relatives,
I recruited my brother and our cousin, Ann.
Pretty Ann, the "baby" and best looking
Among us. In an album of heavy,
Large-boned German faces,
Hers is a pale, foreign polestar.
But *that* day my brother stood nearest the camera:
With his hand held away from him,
He stared where I directed—
Into his shallow palm. And behind him,
Down the narrow driveway,
Impatient and confused, now waving,
Now squinting into the afternoon sun,
Was Ann. I took the picture. Later,

3

When the film came back,
There was my brother with Ann,
An elf in his outstretched hand.

And so photography
Is magic because the eye is.
And tonight I closed one eye and held
A hand up to the stars: none of them
Was larger than a knuckle,
A cluster could have gathered on my nail.
I confess I had forgotten the stars—
But I can remember whole days,
Any number of details when I need to.
Between us—you and me,
Myself and those others
Who live in tall structures—
Between all of us and the stars,
Distance is pure metaphor.
And the cool night is a clear jewel.

August Outing

The spun numbers on the scale blur:
The butcher's weighing the bulk of our lunch,
   The sandwiches we'll eat later—
Lakeside, when we're sun-drenched and hungry.
   What's an outing without food?
And those other summer trappings: blankets

   And basket, lawn chairs, radio.
An inflatable raft, still bloated from the last trip,
   Lies like puffed pastry
In our back seat. And the dashboard looks
   Like a medicine cabinet:
Lip-cream and lotion, you've brought it all.

   Arriving, we light out
For a decent spot: a patch of grass in partial shade,
   Dry as the recent weather.
Far away from the splash of swimmers
   And the roughneck, hulking,
High school kids, playing tackle football,

   We spread our noontime feast,
Lie down as sailboats cut across water.
   But wind blows the thermos over,
And now the quilt your grandmother made
   Is stained with a lousy burgundy.
Though sun washes thought out, I'm serious enough

   To see the links displayed before us:
That frayed and ancient cloth, the picnic basket
   A gift from some out-of-touch friend.

This whole trip seems custom: a shared inheritance,
    A way to pass the summer.
Now the day heats up, sending us in search

    Of drinking water. At the pump
We take turns attending the handle—
    Cupping water, bathing our arms
And reddened faces. At all points we seem
    To intersect with water,
With the tireless trees, the insects that perform

    As they move among flowers.
Once, in the woods that attend the lake, we walked
    Becoming less our talkative selves,
More the silent and passive things we passed:
    Enormous mushrooms, weeds and berries,
We noticed but could not name them.

    This privacy brought us—
Were we rising or sinking?—to the level of sex.
    We wanted to make love. Anxious,
Adolescent, we moved into brush. Unstringing
    Our swimsuits, we lay on a floor
Of grass mixed with gravel. I was of two minds,

    Frightened of being found by the warden
Or, worse, some children lost on an afternoon hike.
    I hovered a moment between two worlds:
To make love almost soundlessly, desire transcending
    The slight inconvenience and pain
Is holy. To do so, and glimpse that we live

    In hope's shadow, moment
To moment, is a subtler grace. It is perfection.

Festival Profile

for Steven

Beyond the damp campgrounds—
To a wide plain that joins the park—
They haul blankets and jugs,
Cameras and stuffed wicker baskets.
Truly a midwestern spring afternoon,
A mild rain lights
On these "friends of the arts,"
Who shoulder the weather and crowd
Three deep to watch the mimes.
This present show seems a love story:
A boy with tears painted on his face
Shyly gives over
A bunch of invisible flowers to his lover
Who takes them and backflips away.
The children love this, clapping
Their hands in fits.

       Happily, no one
Is exchanging money; not even the potters
Are selling their wares. They stay busy
At their wheels, stopping to smoke
Or answer questions. And close by them,
A bearded fellow whittles some beautiful wood,
Carving a one-note instrument
Played like a kazoo.

       Only a few people
Have come to hear the local bards. And over
In the "poetry corner," one finds a handful of girls;
Among them, two boys with their heads bowed.

A large part-German shepherd wanders between
The onlookers and picnic tables
Squared like a barrier around them. In the center,
On the tall grass under a lazy sycamore,
A man calls into a microphone. *Now look,*
He reads from his book, *fibrous sage*
Stunned in the daylight; buds in the open hands
Of the dead. While music, some sort of
Asian music, floats over the man-made lake nearby,
The assembled nod and whisper. It is confusing
And somehow moving, this scene: among many
Odd sounds, a man gestures with both hands,
Trying to be heard; his speech, though not the tone of it,
Lost to those who are apart.

    By five o'clock,
Most have gone home, save some teenagers
Leaning on their cars, drinking beer from bottles.
Long shadows fall across a pavilion
Where two couples cook chicken,
Stooping at times to pick up the paper
Left in the heavily trampled grass. And,
At the far end of the park, a young girl stands
With her emblazoned balloon. From the trees
She turns away—turns from all of us—
Choosing from her coat pocket, among the coins,
A dime for the city bus.

West Pond Road

Wanting
To see the day's events,
She goes out early
In a bright dress. October:
She holds in common
With the birds her graceful
Wakefulness; that, and a certain way
Of holding her head at odd angles.
Under the clearing
Eastern sky, she considers
The play of sun around her.
And what, when she looks long enough,
Does not become personal,
Figurative, sexual? The oak
In the active light and passive shade,
Its leaves dotted yellow.
Behind it, by contrast,
A parody of a tree: winnowed
By frost and strong wind.
What use, she thinks, *are they to me?*
These things which fix her here.
And how is it she can, and
We are all able to turn them—
The quickly changing and the nearly dead—
Into the self: an object of beauty
To love and say so.

The Drowning

Too long the sled has leaned
On the tree. The late light
Of winter draws out the shadows.
A legless upended sofa and two birds
Take the light: beige against
The firewood and dampened garage.
Through the yard, a young boy,
Running into his cluttered
Paradise, releases his lunchbox
With one gloved hand. Behind
The broad tree, the snowy hills—
There, the disfigured crosswise tracks
Go the distance to the river.
The watery ice and his call
As he strikes it, disperse
As the sled tilts, levels, descends.
The boy hears the birds, their swaying
And the sound of pines shaking.
That wind! And everything—
Leaves surfacing and bits of fish—
Becomes cloud-like matter pressing
Forcibly his face, the breathing
That does not carry at all into evening.

The Wake in the Mansion

Death demands little of the one so chosen:
Abstractly among us, involved wholly elsewhere,
He sleeps clean through our fitful vigil.
But among the well-wishers, whom we are,
A need anchored in protocol rises—

We lean over his small wooden boat and stare.
To be looked at and touched, complimented
Without blushing or changing the subject,
That is his privilege. For he is all
The subject of our concern. And it's true

We need not look too deeply there to see
Ourselves: the face in that figure changed,
But no more altered than he now finds himself.
Even the small children sense it: he is
Their mirror, familiar to them, yet somehow strange.

And after a time, we need to be seated.
In a circle we pull up the hardbacked chairs,
(For death *should* involve some discomfort),
To whisper and nod while someone, in a corner,
Weeps mildly and others stop speaking,

Mid-sentence, to remember and dwell on some image
Just come to them: the dead man at a baseball game
After the war; at a neighborhood bar in Chicago
Years later; walking, last week, the hospital corridor.
He didn't look bad, a friend is saying,

Thinking how selfish the body is: demanding,
                              demanding.
And the widow, my aunt, says again *I'll miss him.*
Having closely aligned herself to another,
She has forgotten how to be alone. So what
Comfort will suffice? The priest has an answer:

My uncle has gone to heaven, he tells us.
We *all* want to go to heaven. We are lucky, therefore,
To have someone there, waiting, and on our side.
Explained so simply, I believe his equation.
I remember the stories I read in a book,

Testimonials that could break your heart,
Told by those (as the editor described them)
"Living on borrowed time." Heart attack victims,
A woman pinned in her car by collision,
A teenager who fell from the sky—

Not like a bird, but graceless like Icarus.
Two chutes failed and he sank to his knees
In concrete, and outside the Plaza Shopping Center.
As if he were trying to enter the earth!
He could not do it. And he did not die.

Those who have "passed away" and passed back again,
Report one common occurrence: friends and family—
Already dead—came at waking's end to meet them.
Those veteran dead took the victims' hands,
And tugging some, helped them rise out of their bodies.

Who can argue with stories like these? They're
Hopeful and colorful. I know myself that the pull
To stay alive is great, and work with attention,
Uneven attention, to give up the self-denying habits
I own: they would have me be, too quickly, stone.

And I don't want to be as you have become
And are now, Uncle. Your name is my middle name.
Soon it will be evening, time to drive home
In the year's first snow—already turning—
Warming to slush on the highway.

Your death works to magnify our understanding:
Dying, one man is gone. Though our hearts enlarge,
Our daily weathers remain about the same.
Goodbye: we go home to talk and suffer,
To distance ourselves from you over supper.

Marble

Towards evening from the fields
The birds rose up, their flight
Like an ordinary object of desire.
But as was your way, you kept going.
The landscape flashing past,
This interested you: how the full eye
Acknowledged yet could not contain it.

In the figures passing—
Young boys in shirt sleeves,
Cyclists riding in twos through town—
You sensed a reluctance so that
Their voices, no longer remote,
Involved you. Overhead, a balcony;
Bunches of late-summer roses on a table.

What value the scene held
Was in its transparency. For a moment,
Your head cleared; you hoped there
Might be no end to it. Yet the poles
Between which you wandered appeared
To have allegorical tags;
Sun and moon; north, south; green
And deeper green. You were looking

For something still. At the avenue's end,
A statue—the lines in marble cut
A willful middle distance between crucial
And merely useful. Was that it? Or had
The walk been just easy? Later, as the wind
Rocked shut the garden gate, you again
Began setting right these distinctions.

Resting

Adrift
On an oversized pillow—
A girl resting.
Or rather
A woman with her eyes
Newly opened.
Clean linen washes
White over one breast.
In this basement studio,
She gives over her attention
To desire. In sleep
She does the same.
The walls are the color
Of earth, *are* earth,
And like the red
Dresser
And crowded nightstand,
Matter to her only
As a generous
Confusion of color. I
Cannot say she is
Convalescing; perhaps
It is just evening.
It seems there is a moisture
In the air
That makes her skin shine,
The bedclothes
Cling
About those heavy
Shoulders. And the light
Showing her face
Holds not its appearance

So much as her look.
What bends the olive tree,
Bowing at the window?
The new rain makes
The dull fruit glow.
Why does the breeze
Come down to join her
In that closed surround?

A Virtue of Shape

The woman let her hand trail
In the water. With her fingers
She drew lines, representing waves.
Other waves the boat made, passing
Close to shore through the water
That was cold and clear. The evening
Coming on was a part of what she saw,
And the man across from her, rowing.

What could spoil such a lovely ride?
She let her hand trail in the water.
The boat continued, and the fish
Below. The wind picked up a little.
Had she noticed them before—
The wind at odd intervals,
The bluefish heading into shore?
It didn't matter: the ride would continue
And night arrive. Eventually,
Against the border of sky,
One element would stand out to speak
The weight of these things: meaning
Being a virtue of shape and order.

The Young Couple

Summer was slow in coming on:
Twice they had abandoned plans
For vacation. Now, kept home,
They quarreled and were withdrawn
From one another. On the sofa
That late afternoon, she combed

Her hair and thought of the cliffs
Near her parents' cabin. She had
Loved the jack pines there, the daily rain.
Plotless, these images pleased her.
Meanwhile, across the room,
Her young husband sat by the fan

That turned on the wooden table.
What was it about him? Even his voice
Annoyed her as she stared out
At the painted trees, automobiles,
Complexly angled poles and wires:
A choice display of dull particulars

On which she could not focus, feeling
Nothing for it. She must have it wrong,
She thought: summer's famous
Changes would not help them. Or was
Any wash of memory a darkened address
From where one sees the present? Always less.

Rilke at Worpswede

Germany, 1901

Past midnight the first morning air
Seemed to go to their heads:
They remarked to one another
How suddenly it was cooler,
Although it was not. And only
He remained apart, having argued
With an older man. Who made the brave
Strokes of brush and palette knife
On the canvas that hung above them?

At the piano Milly sang Schubert again:
O gracious Art, in many a darkling hour . . .
A maudlin piece, but the girls!
(How for him—such radiant and commanding
Angels—they posed difficult, critical problems.)
They leaned on the sill, these girls
In white dresses, looking out at the night
Where the moon was silvering the poplars.

Later, after a long time drinking,
The room came alive
With their youthful movement.
And in the midst of dancing,
He did not dance, but gazed at them dumbly
Or talked, in one corner, to Clara—
So quietly she leaned forward to hear him—
Already thinking of the walk
Back under a vault of new stars
To his small but well-lighted studio.

II

Journal

In another time, I could look outside
With a kind of white envy,
An endlessly impatient gaze.
The sunny lawns, the line of houses
With triangular porches,
A neighbor's long-handled shovel—
I admired these things
For their simple vanity:
A gift of function and place.
And all that I saw seemed a temptation—
Even the maples called out
For more than my observation.

Complicity is what the world offered
When I was seventeen. Desire
Was a way of measuring the self,
That feeling off-center
That made me write angrily in my journal.
Alone, I'd map out a small plan
For tomorrow. But when tomorrow came,
I'd sit on the porch,
A boy in tennis shoes and thick sunglasses,
Waiting for my father to come home.

Nothing ever really changes,
I wrote in that red ink.
Deciphering the oversized scrawl—
Unread these fifteen years—
Memory allows me to trace a path
From this day to that. What will
Let me forgive my nervous inwardness?
Anchored to home, the hours passed,

Although something in me longed to be out.
I feel it even now, a heady desire,
As a newspaper drifts across the lawn
And catches in the thorn bush beginning to blossom.

City Pool

The afternoon is a lonely place
And I know the signs: the sun
Angling down on these aging brides
Who sit, paired up at poolside,
With drugstore novels in their hands.
Their children flap along the deck,
Except for the few who float, faceup,
With jackets strapped to their chests.
No one breathes easily this heavy air—
Least of all, the old men.
They lie on their sides or flat
On their backs with heads
Propped on wadded-up towels and t-shirts.
Though they look half dead,
The lifeguards don't notice them—
They're too busy scouting
The diving area, waiting for someone
To break his head as he stumbles
Off the high-board. Surely it's no accident
That a gaggle of pale girls
Are all wearing the tiniest
Of flowered bikinis and carrying
Enormous radios. They strain
Against the rusting chainlink fence,
While the boys stand talking in a circle.
Water has brought us together,
And the light is almost bright enough
To blur distinctions of age and grace.
The afternoon is a lonely place:
We rise up into the present moment,
Shimmering, surprised again by the sun
Which treats us as we treat ourselves—
Not badly, but with a human indifference.

Sunbathers

In a clearing
Among yellow pine—resting
Or walking and turning away—
The bathers notice
Nothing so small as the ants
On the rocks and flat places.
In this powerful light
What does not shine?—
And shining, become indistinct
As the eye sees it. The bathers
Pay no attention: their eyes
Mostly closed now even to each other,
In this place far from water.
And how must they feel
In this slowed-down time?
Heavy with heat, it is likely
They are almost thoughtless.
The big-breasted women
Stretch awkwardly out
Near the men who are naked
And ape-like. Yet perched
On the grassy land there is one
Who imagines himself an Adonis.
And he is, for a moment,
Like the clear, ice-capped mountains
In the distance behind him,
As handsome, painted and strange.

Waking at Night

It would be easy to dismiss them—
They're bored, I'd say,
Meaning those people across the alley
Who gather past midnight, alone or in pairs,
At the all-night convenience store.
And some of them probably are.
Under hell's own rinsed-out lighting,
They bump down the submarine aisles,
Looking for something to eat or drink,
Something to put on a scratch
Or take home to a pet.
Searching gives them something to do,
But not much and not for long:
The clerk keeps asking, *Hi, can I help you?*—
Knowing damn well no one can.
Not tonight, anyway, in this condition.

Who am I to judge them? My own window opens
To the street and those teenagers
Racing their cars by the pumps.
There's a tree gone numb with the resting weight
Of birds that come nightly to nest.
I don't know what I expected to see,
But those shapes like high-flung stones
Are disturbing, crowded in sagging rows.
Earlier, in bed, I dozed a while
But rose before some dream could take me;
A churning in my stomach signaled
Some fear, but nothing I could locate or name.
That's how the unconscious speaks to us—
Cast adrift, a message bobs in our sluggish blood
With a warning to keep awake, keep watchful.

The worst can happen, don't we all know it,
And probably already has—
If not to me, then to one
Of these neighbors I keep my sleepy eye on.

Sunnyside Drive, 1960

Eleven years neighbors,
Sisters for forty, my mother loved "Aunt Bets."
Aunt's hair, a misshapen globe,
Was an elaborate, trademarked affair—
Much the style of the time.
Bleached white weekly at *Kut & Kurl,*
A cut-rate "school for beauty,"
She came home Saturdays
And mooned by the mirror until dinner.
She was no longer a girl:
Luminous and chatty, portly in her pedal pushers,
She knocked about the kitchen.

No longer a girl! Nor was my mother.
Younger, she married late in 1948,
One year after her sister.
Betty had Frank; now mother, William.
Frank was a muscular bore whom mother
Remembers as early as '42—
"He used to stop by on his motorcycle,
Late in the evening when he got off work.
It was during the war; he had bad feet
Or something. All the good men were gone."

Now these four adults
Spent their leisure time together.
Mother was the instigator,
A do-gooder killing time on the phone.
Concerned, indiscriminate,
She involved them all in charity—
Catholic Missions, Easter Seals, Unicef.
Bored still, she started a bridge club.

Night after night then, they camped in the basement—
My aunt exhausted, my uncle exhausted,
My poker-faced father pale and attentive
While mother referred to the rules.
Still a joking boy, my uncle stacked
His cardboard chips, suggested playing for cigarettes.
Father said nothing, looking over his cigar.

Even in photographs taken at the time,
My father seems to recede.
One Halloween, on mother's suggestion,
They went to a bash at the Moose Lodge.
The snapshot is muddy,
Metaphoric, underexposed:
In blackface and beat-up shoes,
Betty and Frank bookend my parents.
Mother and father are living-room Indians:
All leather trimmings and washable war paint,
My father's face lost
In a turkey-feathered headdress.
The sequence shot has them leaving—
The ladies packed in the back of father's
Rust-colored Buick Deluxe.

The next day was All Saints.
Planes from the airport roared overhead
As Betty sidestepped pumpkins and eggs.
Mother stooped to save crepe paper.

Sister and sister,
They walked their kids to school.

Man Waxing Car, 1954

Father bends forward to polish the grille,
And small flecks
Of dirt darken his shoes,
Darken the pavement below them.

On the porch in the afternoon air,
His wife waits—my mother,
Cigarette in hand. She sighs,

Exhaling a screen of smoke
Which rises above her and hangs there.
He stands on tiptoe to rub
Down the roof. Behind him, the sky is mild.

Now my mother is nodding while father talks.
She leans back
And, with all her heart, believes him.

Fragments from a Childhood

1954–57, 1983

My Irish grandfather,
Dead twenty years, passes his hand
Over my face in a gesture
Which signals the start
Of the game. He tugs with two fingers
At the bridge of my nose.
My eyes close and, when I look again,
My nose seems to be in his fist—
A pink thing, upturned.
He shakes it at me, saying,
It's mine now, Tommy. Will you look at this!

It's a game I play with him
Because he enjoys it. What I enjoy
Is living away from my parents—
If only for several weeks each summer—
Free to waste time as I want.
Sitting in a fan-shaped chair,
I stare down at Avenue E,
At the stores that the people
Pass through in their lunchtime hurry.
Nights I hear the El go by,
Squealing on its tangle of tracks.
It stops at a stop by the bedroom
And the brakes rasp;
The doors come open with a shudder.

My grandfather shudders in his sleep.
I lie beside him, sucking my fingers,
Hoping tonight I won't wet the bed.

Right now, the room has my grandfather's smell,
Something I connect with the shade
That rots on the window,
The window so small it allows
Just one wedge of moonlight through,
Shining in my face when I move my head . . .

Thirty years later,
These same scenes are piecemeal,
Possibly remembered wrongly.
I play them over in my head
To establish a point of view:
I *was* that child in a city apartment,
The boy in thick glasses
In photographs my mother owns.
I've spliced them together—
These photographs to anecdotes
I've been told. And now they flicker:
My grandfather conjured back,
Animated, on a roll,
As if this concentrated
Attention to memory
Could make him live again, whole.

Then

All that morning in their house
I had been sleeping on a shapeless pillow,
Dreaming of my mother in her nightgown.
It was winter and a white room. Elsewhere,
The sounds of a large dog barking
And the pipes, the water in them,
Filling up and letting go.
My mother and I on a sofa sat so close,
We touched and were perfectly weightless.
Her hands, when I felt them, were quite cold.

Because her eyes were closed, I believed
She was thinking: some things random,
Perhaps, confused as her breathing,
Its queer measure. When I looked at her,
She said *it is so quiet,* but she was wrong.
In what little light there was, her face
Was charged and divided. She held
In her arms my small body. Then,
Above the dog's whine, a door slammed
And I woke wanting conversation.

But in the kitchen I could see
She had been arguing again.
The wind was up already; it was afternoon.
And he was gone whom my mother
Had never loved, and I was glad.

In the Park, Considering Parenthood

I

Below us the swings are empty:
   They tap in the wind
     And make a hollow sound
That carries—not far, a little way
   Up the ridge or beyond—
     To the grassy place
Where we are walking. You and I,
   In late October,
     Have arrived at least
Two weeks too late; it's past the time
   When the maples—not full—
     Are still most beautiful.
And it's easy to imagine—here
   In this park which borders
     The highway—
We're part of the tired argument:
   City and nature, separate poles
     With their strong pulls.
Above us, a bird calls twice,
   And we see its nest—
     Exposed, too photogenic—
Is larger than we would have guessed.
   Should we pass back over
     The bridge that passes
Over the milky, narrow stream?
   It leads—if we follow
     Long enough—to four
Or five expensive, ancient houses.

II

Beyond the gravel bicycle path—
    The building that houses
        The local Art Center
And Museum of Modern Science. An easy irony!
    Or, maybe, as the planners
        Saw it, "the best of both worlds."
Time to climb down from this spot
    To see, as planned,
        If the museum is open.
Well, it is, but we're out of luck—
    Two dollars a person
        And neither of us thought
To bring money. We might barter
    With the ticket-taker,
        But would it be worth the effort?
Looking through the wall-sized window,
    We see what would welcome us:
        The pint-sized swinging
Pendulum, the slightly larger globe
    Of the world, and next
        To it that dark twin—
A poorly done mock-up: relief of the moon.
    Down the corridor,
        A sign we can make out
If we squint, the two of us
    Slowly reciting: *The*
        Phone . . . Of . . . The . . . Future.
Childless, we agree this is a place
    To bring children.

III

At the back of the building, almost hidden,
    We find a one-room school.
        We press our faces
To the window, cupping our hands to cut the glare.
    More surprising changes of scale—
        Below us, on the windowsill,
A box of miniature scissors with dull,
    Rounded edges. Can these really
        Cut through paper? And crayons
In a container, oversized, the kind
    A kid can wrap a hand around.
        Artificial, a dozen dazzling colors:
Sea Green, Cinnamon. My favorite's
    Purple Passion. These would look more
        At home a little farther
Up this slope, next to the Oldenburg "Eraser."
    There's also a mysterious jar,
        Holding something we can't
Make out, something living or formerly alive,
    Hinted at by a makeshift lid,
        The pinholes punched in tinfoil.
And high over the heads
    Of twenty dwarf desks
Is a ledge that bridges three walls.
    Displayed there, arranged in a row,
        Giant flashcards: each
Holds a letter of the alphabet,
    Printed with an illustration.
        H has a drawing of a hat on it,
W drags a wagon, *C* has a cat curled inside,
    F—What is that supposed to be?—
        I guess it's someone's father.

But that man's younger than I am—
   He's practically a kid
      With a pipe for a prop,
Another reminder of how, at times,
   The world conforms so that
      Each thing takes on
The weight we want. We walk back
   A zigzag path
      To the car, heading towards home
And soon into winter,
   Talking, tapping under our feet
      The dying leaves and shining needles . . .

III

March

Here is a lawn, textured
   As in needlepoint,
A place for this student
   To exercise
His Golden Retriever. And there,
   Beyond the cars

Passing, birds startle
   And the wind
Lifts the spiked branches
   Of spruce . . .
I see what I want to
   In this endless

Present. Now the boy bends,
   Touching his toes;
The afternoon flames to a close.
   What sense of myself
Can possibly matter in moments
   Clear as these? My heartbeat's

Aligned to the sparrow's
   Upward motion—
Not an arc exactly, but more
   The spiral palpitations
Of a football in flight.
   I'm trying to set

These images down right,
   But looking out
From my second-floor window,
   I'm not sure
What I understand, or should.
   There's only a sense

Of random connections. Now
   When I look
Again out the window,
   It is evening.
The light's failing
   Is tempered by

My own sense of wasted time.
   Why don't I do something?
Back on the lawn, the boy
   Has been joined
By some friends, and the dog
   Has moved

A few lots down the street.
   But the bushes
Seem shot through with color—
   A blue
I hadn't noticed before.
   Can I say it is

A *luminous* blue? And that
   As it shines,
It mirrors the day's losses,
   Fading to purple
In the porchlight coming on?

Autumnal

What was it that
  Struck me as curious
    On the road, returning home?
It was late afternoon,
  Cold for September, so
    I had the heater
Turned on in the car: it gave off
  That chemical odor
    Machines make after long rest.
The trees, I noticed,
  Had not yet begun
    To turn as the light had.
Against the roughly cut,
  Overlapping buildings—
    Creating a modest skyline—
The light was angled and going out
  Earlier than I last remembered.
    I'd just had my hair cut
At the airport. I was thinking
  Of physical comfort:
    A bath and shave,
Sitting down to supper.
  But the road became strange
    As I passed by water.
  Cars in the distance
Crossed the bridge in a line—
  Over the Iowa River, rising,
    All of us coming home.
Home, then, in my comfortable study,
  I tried to get that
    Feeling down. I urged it on,

But could only write: *Today*
   The light pointed
     Towards something important.
Or was it the water?
  I verged on understanding
    And was stalled.

The North Farms

We rode our bicycles
  In the late afternoon,
    Four curving miles.
Fields there and farm lands
  Opened out: it was more
    Visibly autumn. On those
Hole-ridden roads,
  The metal fenders rang;
    The wind, encumbered,
Blew crosswise
  Through a thicket of aspen,
    Towards the deep
Ditches on either side.
  What buildings there were—
    Sheds and a few barns
Leaning on cone-heavy jack pines—
  Appeared merely decorative.
    Who built them
Like that, left them so completely
  To weather?

      Farther
  From us, a block or more
Down a gravel path,
  Were three houses. Stopping
    To look through
The ruined picture windows,
  We guessed others
    Had gone in to root
Through the clutter—
  Umbrellas with no handles,
    A dogbowl, candles;

On an oversized sofa,
　　The shell of a radio.
　　　Did this collection
Say anything important? True,
　　We leave behind
　　　What we can no longer bear
To exhibit or own—
　　The worn-out and gone-useless.
　　We agreed on the cliché,
Saying that the families
　　Who lived here once
　　　Had "changed for the better."

Again and quietly, the leaves
　　Came lightly down. And
　　　I saw you looked tired now,
Turning to go home. It would seem
　　A longer haul back,
　　　I knew: I had been
To that place sometimes
　　Without you. Then
　　　A large bird called
Down to us from its high tree,
　　Which was already
　　　Quite bare. And the sound
Carried in the chill
　　Evening air, supported
　　　By our presence.

In the Late Spring, Cutting Tulips

for Mark

Snap them off at the necks.
The tulips will come back
Brighter next year,
Double if you splice them right.

Today, when I cut those flowers,
The petals seemed to swell
Before they finally broke open.
I thought about the day you moved away.
On the porch, you pointed
To this simple garden,
Then walked a straight line
From my house to your car.
You were wearing a white hat,
As though already it were summer.

Last summer I read *The Book of Names:*
Lily, Rose, Alex, Ambrose . . .
My wife was newly pregnant.
From books I learned
How children learn. They discover
That objects removed from sight—
Rattle, bottle, a favorite shoe—
Don't stop being
And can, in time, be recovered.

Today, from the lawn,
I recovered a branch
Caught in last night's storm.
I watched an ant

47

Cross over the tossed-down tulips—
White Candle, Arabian Night,
I said their names to myself.
While the sun eased
Out of a slow-moving cloud,
I floated above my minor sadness
And believed that the flowers
Would come back double,
That I would see you again.

Measure: For Jacob

In the last months, in utero,
the baby may respond to light and sound. . . .
—Complete Childbirth Book

Sprawled on the sofa
In the quiet afternoon,
An ear to my wife's swollen navel . . .
How must we look to the postman
Who passes our window?
He's late because of the rain.
The rain beats down on the tulips,
On the strawberries
Making a small start,
And the grass grown so tall
We don't walk through it.

We're not going anywhere now:
I'm attending the school
For soon-to-be-fathers,
Listening hard for the unborn's heartbeat,
Hoping to feel movement—
Swimming or a slight kick.
This is the music of sweet waiting,
As the rain strokes the windows.

Later, coming down from my study,
I find her drowsing—
A cord from the stereo
Extends to the headphones
She's placed on her stomach.
Now when I place my ear there,
I'm rewarded with a ghostly flutter—

A noise like the whirring
In outer space,
Like static on the receiver.

Maybe this proves what the book explains:
The body's a string, a waxy wire
Two kids with cans can talk through.
Like the hairs in the ear
That measure the tone of sudden emotion,
Our voices rising in happiness or pain,
The skin gives just enough
To let us hear *your* music.

So if we're impatient for you to arrive,
That's because, long ago,
You set out like light
From a faraway star. And if
Music is sound passing in time,
Then light's a measure also,
A kind of music we can see through
Almost to the future.

The Music Box

In the next room,
   Because the music box
     Plays this single tune,
My wife is singing
   "Happy Birthday." She sings
     To our son, but

Of course it's not his birthday.
   Nor anyone else's we know.
     It's just a gloomy Saturday
In the middle of March,
   A light snow falling
     And the cold slowly killing

The tulips which started
   Too early this year.
     My wife's high voice
Fills the sleepy air,
   As she changes
     The second couplet:

Happy birthday to you,
   She sings again,
     You look like a monkey
And you smell like one, too.
   It's a kid's silly version,
     Picked up twenty years ago,

Recited, then as now, to tease.
   It has no effect at all on Jacob.
     He's ten months old,

And only this odd box
   Holds his attention,
      Chiming and spinning

Three tiny figures around.
   There's a boy
      Holding a blue balloon
And a girl holding
   A green one. Their companion,
      A dog of indeterminate breed,

Winds clockwise between them.
   How could they not be happy?
      This handsomely crafted
Circle of friends . . .
   Frozen there, they have
      Only one task:

Respond to the key's release.
   Now, as they track
      Their given course—
Their painted faces,
   The size of thumbnails,
      Fixed permanently in grins—

Jacob is speechless,
   But my wife continues to sing.
      Monkeys and zoos,
Candles, balloons,
   We can name these emblems
      Of childhood, but not

What they called up in us:
   The complex sensations
      That often left us stunned.

Singing to others,
  We sing for ourselves.
    My wife's voice, the absurd lyric,

Carry her back—and me with her—
  To the wooden past, those
    Mornings I heard
Someone singing my own name:
  My young mother calling,
    Calling me back

From that childhood sleep
  Which is itself
    A kind of perfect music.

Rounds

In the blue distance, an orange speck:
The paperboy at afternoon's end.
That sack he wears over his shoulder
Is "day-glo," hoisted like a warning flag
And visible for blocks. And he is too—

Visible by implication. As autumn implies
Dying, it is left to us to imagine him:
Doubled up under that pulpous, inky weight.
Now he shortcuts the long corner,
Crossing the well-kept but leafy lawn

Of the First Lutheran Trinity Church.
No doubt he's memorized his route by now,
The zigzag six-block round he makes,
Always more interested in the daily distractions
Than in this job he's lately taken on.

Today's action includes: two girls, young,
Their arms filled with groceries,
Struggling up a drive; then a runner comes
Towards him in a striped-blue sweatsuit.
And a yellow spaniel follows at his feet

Or runs ahead and waits. He is lost in thought.
That's why he still misses our house.
It's new on the route, and he hasn't
Got it down yet. My complaining to his boss
Will no doubt fix that, sooner or later,

But meanwhile I feel a measure of guilt.
Do I ask too much? Still that seems

To be how it works: some light pressure
Is applied, prodding us into remembering.
And seeing him has such an effect on me.

Watching the birds flutter down from the trees—
Made miniature by the great gulf of air
Between us—it could be ten years from now:
This child my own son, daughter.
Or twenty years back! I was that boy,

Getting up early for three-fifty a week.
Jobs are earned admittance into the miserly,
Ordinary world. As evidence, here I am:
Thinking to write down something of autumn.
His art, I see now, reminds me of my own—

Balancing memory with expectation.
The long perspective deepens. Past, future:
We guess from what surrounds us,
Though they extend over the horizon endlessly.
It is enough to have our rounds to make,

Sometimes entering the lives of others,
Sometimes with such precision! Outside
The Trinity Church, a lighted sign
Comes on with the evening, blinking
The weekly warning: *Redemption Center:*

No Stamps Needed For Your Full Reward.
So much floating up into our field of vision,
Catching the eye, demanding attention,
Demanding the mind make anything it touches its own.
The way a sparrow, diving, goes

Under the paperboy's overhand toss,
Our allegiance and those objects

All head into evening. And the paper
Is headed towards someone else's porch,
A neighbor I hardly know. I let it go.

At the Botanical Center

July 1, 1984

Today, on a narrow walkway,
    Stalled in a crawling
Line of onlookers, I stood
    Before a banana tree
That bloomed in the heat.
    In the press of bodies—
Full sun slanting through
    The glass dome above us—
My vision blurred . . . And

In that dreamy instant,
A deepening feeling
    Let me see
The tree for what is was—
    Exotic and beautiful,
Lonely in this place. So I
    Was glad to belong
In the company of tourists,
    Strangers   touching

The green shoots of living things.
    On the eve of another
Birthday, I made my given wish:
    To become less
Like the one tree, more like
    The local florae.
Beneath the knee-high signs
    That named them,
Those smaller wonders were
    Indistinguishable,
Growing close together on the ground.